Aa

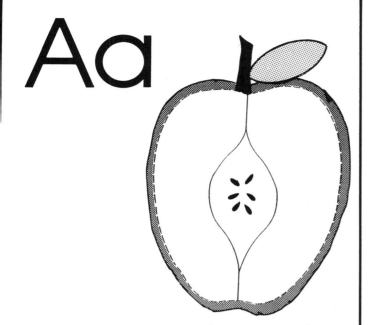

Read it!

1. *Ed Emberley's ABC* by Ed Emberly
2. *Apple Pigs* by Ruth Orbach
3. *I Can't Said The Ant*
   by Polly Cameron

Eat it!

Applesauce

(for 3 cups)

2 pounds tart cooking apples
1/2-2/3 cup sugar (depends on tartness of the apples)
1/2 cup water

1. Wash, core, and pare the apples; cut into quarters.
2. Put water into a saucepan. Bring to a boil, add apples, and bring back to a boil.
3. Reduce heat, simmer 20-25 minutes. Stir occasionally. Add water if needed.
4. Stir in sugar until well combined. Serve warm or cold.

Enjoy applesauce with animal crackers and milk.

Draw it!

Direct students to fold a blank piece of paper into four sections. Draw on the chalkboard or use oral instructions to guide students to draw the following:

1. Make a red ant.
2. Make an angry red ant.
3. Make a red ant on a green leaf.
4. Make a red ant going uphill.

Oral language Experience:
   Students dictate a sentence or short story about one of the pictures to an adult.

Make it!

An Appetizing Apple

Outside Apple Pattern

Cover this section before reproducing.

Materials:

- Reproduce the pattern on this page on red, green, or yellow construction paper.

- Reproduce the pattern on the following page on white construction paper.

- Scissors and paste

- 1" x 2½" brown construction paper for a stem.

- 2" x 3" green construction paper for a leaf

- Optional: real apple seeds

Steps to follow:

1. Cut out both apple patterns.

2. Paste the inside of the apple on the outside of the apple leaving a colored border.

3. Cut a leaf from the green rectangle. Paste the leaf to the brown stem.

4. Paste the stem on the back of the apple.

5. Color the seeds brown or glue on real apple seeds.

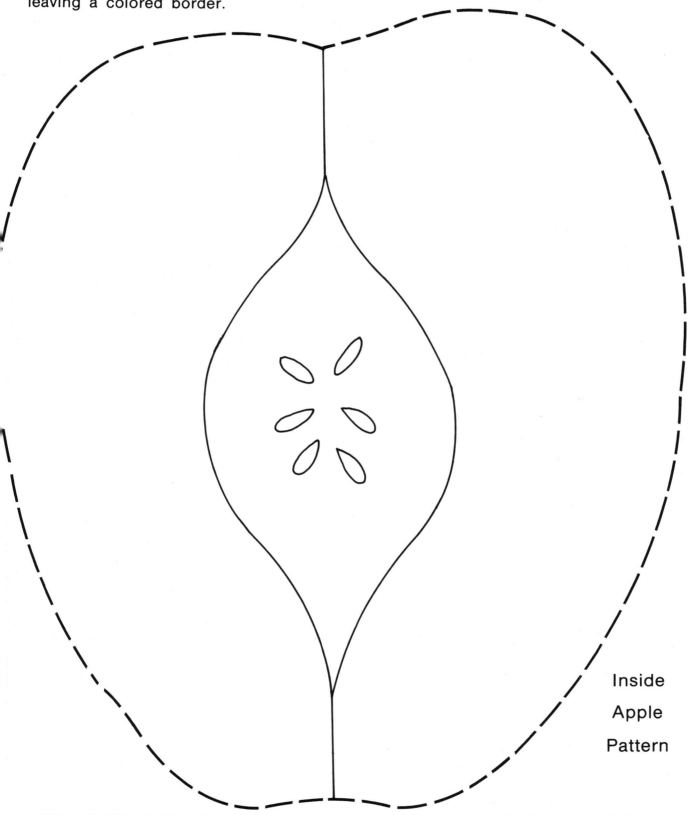

Inside

Apple

Pattern

Bb

Read it!

1. *Ben's ABC Day* by Terry Berger and Alice Kendell
2. *Corduroy* by Don Freeman
3. *Everything Has A Shape And Everything Has A Size* by Bernice Kohn

Eat it!
Butter and Bread

Make butter
    1 pint whipping cream
    1 quart jar and lid
    Yellow food coloring
    Salt to taste

1. Pass the jar of whipping cream around the room, letting each child shake it 20 times. Add salt and coloring when it is the consistency of whipped cream. Continue until a lump of butter forms.
2. Rinse the butter in cold water until the water is clear.

Have a bread tasting party with your homemade butter.

toast	rye crisp	tortilla
bagel	cornbread	scone

Draw it!

Direct students to fold a blank piece of paper into four sections. Draw on the chalkboard or use oral instructions to guide students to draw the following:

1. Make a big, bouncy red balloon.
2. Make a beautiful, little blue balloon.
3. Make two balloons. One is purple and one is orange.
4. Make a big yellow balloon with red polka dots.

Oral language Experience:
    Students dictate a sentence or short story about one of the pictures to an adult.

Make it!

Bears Bears Bears

Make charming polar bears and brown bears from this easy pattern. It can also easily become a panda. (Be sure to explain to your students that a panda is not a bear.)

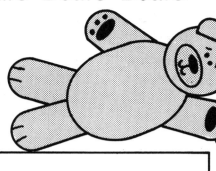

Materials:

For all bears:

- Scissors, paste
- Black marker or crayon

For Brown Bear:

- Dark construction paper:
  4- 3" x 6" for legs
  2- 2" squares for ears
  1- 5" square for head
  1- 6" x 9" for body

- Light brown construction paper:
  1- 2½" x 3" for muzzle

For Polar Bear:

- White construction paper:
  4- 3" x 6" for legs
  2- 2" squares for ears
  1- 5" square for head
  1- 6" x 9" for body

For Panda:

- Black construction paper:
  4- 3" x 6" for legs
  2- 2" squares for ears

- White construction paper:
  1- 5" square for head
  1- 6" x 9" for body

Note—all the bears' bodies are made the same way. The faces are different.

1. Round the 5" square into a circle head.

    Round the 6" x 9" into an oval body.

    Round one end only of the 2- 2" square ears and the 4- 3" x 6" legs.

2. Paste the bear together:

    Paste the head on the body.

    Paste the ears on top of the head.

    Paste the "arms" and legs on the back side of the bear with the rounded edges forming paws.

Steps to follow:

3. Brown Bear only:

    Round the 2½" x 3" light brown paper into an oval. Paste the oval on the face to create a muzzle.

4. Use black marker or black crayon to add details.

    Paws for brown and polar bears

Faces: You will want to demonstrate step by step how to make the facial features.

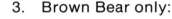

Polar Bear   Brown Bear   Panda

Hint: Create a cute hanging decoration for your room by stapling the bears paw to paw to make bear chains.

Cc

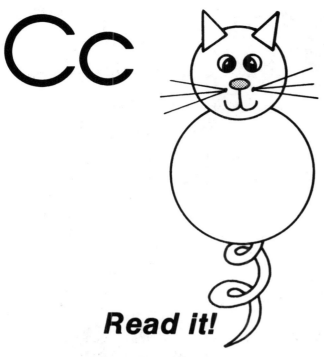

Read it!

1. *Animal Alphabet* by Ben Kitchen
2. *The Knitted Cat* by Antonella Bolliger-Savelli
3. *If You Give A Mouse A Cookie* by Laura Joffe Numeroff

Eat it!

Cool Custard

Prepare packaged custard mix or your favorite custard recipe.

Try some warm cocoa with your cool custard.

Draw it!

Direct students to fold a blank piece of paper into four sections. Draw on the chalkboard or use oral instructions to guide students to draw the following:

1. Make a chocolate chip cookie.
2. Make a peanut butter cookie.
3. Make a smiling cookie.
4. Make a cookie with a bite out of it.

Oral language Experience:
   Students dictate a sentence or short story about one of the pictures to an adult.

Make it!

Crazy Cross-eyed Cat

This cute cat gives a lot of practice in cutting circles and gives you the opportunity to teach how to cut a spiral.

Materials:

- Choose any color construction paper and cut:

  1- 9" square for body
  2- 6" squares for head and tail

- 2- 2" squares of yellow construction paper for eyes (choose another color if you are making yellow cats)

- 1- 1' x 1½" in a contrasting color for the nose

- Long pine needles for whiskers (or use yarn cut in 3" lenghts, long toothpicks, broomstraws, etc.)

- Scissors, paste, crayons

- Glue

Steps to follow:

1. Round the 9" square and the 2- 6" squares into circles. Save 2 corner scraps to use for ears.

2. Paste the head onto the body. Add the scraps you saved to create ears.

3. Cut the tail circle into a spiral. Paste one end of the spiral on the bottom of the back side of the body.

4. Round the 2- 2" squares into eyes and the 1" x 1½" piece into an oval nose. Paste on the cat's face.

5. Use crayon to draw the mouth and color in the crossed eyes.

6. Glue on pine needles, yarn, toothpicks, or broomstraws for whiskers. (Paste is not enough to hold the whiskers in place.)

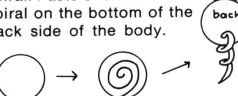

Hint: To display these cats, punch holes in the top of each head. Tie on strings and hang the cats around the room.

Dd

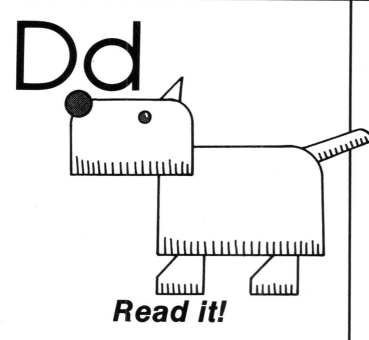

Read it!

1. *An Edward Lear Alphabet*
   by Edward Lear
2. *Angus* by Marjorie Flack
3. Check your A-V catalog for the film
   of Robert McCloskey's book
   Homer Price

Eat it!

Doughnuts and "Dragon's" Milk

Recipe for dragon's milk:
1. Put milk in a pan.
2. Warm the milk.
Or...get a dragon to breathe on it!

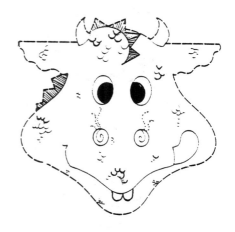

Draw it!

Direct students to fold a blank piece of
paper into four sections. Draw on the
chalkboard or use oral instructions to
guide students to draw the following:

1. Make a delicious doughnut.
2. Make a dunking doughnut
   with red sprinkles.
3. Make a doughnut hole.
4. Make a blueberry doughnut
   with a bite out of it.

Oral language Experience:
   Students dictate a sentence or short
story about one of the pictures to an
adult.

Make it!

Dudley, the **D**apper **D**og

Use this dog to teach your children to cut fringe.

Materials:

- Use 1- 12" x 18" or 2- 12" x 9" sheets of black construction paper to cut these sizes:

  1- 9" x 12" for body
  1- 6" x 9" for head
  1- 5" square for feet
  1- 1½" x 4" for tail

- Brown construction paper:

  1- 1" square for eye
  1-, 2" square for nose

- Scissors, paste

Steps to follow:

1. Round one corner of the 9" x 12" black for the body.

   Round the 2 top corners of the 6" x 9" black for the head.

   Save a scrap from the body to make an ear.

2. Fringe the bottom edge of the body and head by making small cuts (about 1" long) with the tip of the scissors.

   Note- these are irregular cuts at irregular intervals.

3. Paste the head on the square unfringed corner of the body.

4. Use the scrap you saved from the body to cut a triangular ear. Paste the ear on the head.

5. To make feet:

   Fold the 5" square in half diagonally. Open the paper and cut on the fold.

   Hold the triangle this way and cut off the bottom tip.

   Fringe the bottom.

   Repeat for the other foot.

   Paste the feet to the back side of the body.

   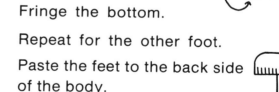

7. Make a tail by rounding off one top corner of the 1½" x 4" black paper.

   Fringe the bottom by using small cuts.

8. Paste the tail in place on the back side of the dog.

9. Round the 2" brown square into a circle for the nose and the 1" square into a circle for the eye.

   Paste the pieces in place. The nose sticks out beyond the edge of the head.

Ee

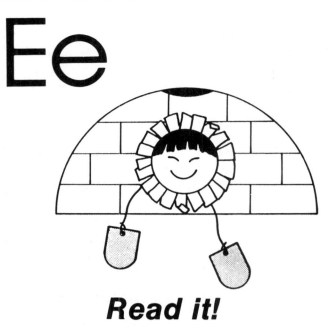

Read it!

1. *Babar's ABC*
   by Laurent De Brunhoff
2. *On Mother's Lap*
   by Ann Herbert Scott
3. *Chickens Aren't The Only Ones*
   by Ruth Heller

Eat it!

Eat chilly Eskimo Pie ice cream bars.

Discussion: Why do you think these ice cream bars are called Eskimo pies?

Draw it!

Direct students to fold a blank piece of paper into four sections. Draw on the chalkboard or use oral instructions to guide students to draw the following:

1. Make a small, blue robin's egg.
2. Make a large, brown chicken's egg.
3. Make a chicken's egg with a crack.
4. Make a hard-boiled egg with a yellow yolk.

Oral language Experience:
   Students dictate a sentence or short story about one of the pictures to an adult.

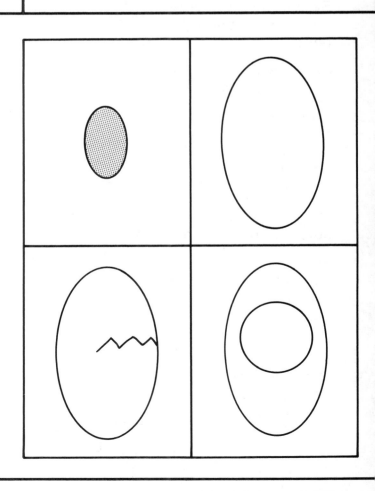

Make it!

Edgar, the Energetic Eskimo

This little Eskimo will never be without mittens because he keeps them on a string around his neck.

Materials:

- Blue construction paper for the igloo   9" x 12"

- White construction paper for the Eskimo's parka 5" x 5"

- Light brown construction paper for the Eskimo's face 3" x 3"

- Red construction paper for mittens   5" x 3½"

- 12" piece of yarn for mitten string

- Scissors, crayons and, paste

- Hole punch

Steps to follow:

1. Fold the blue construction paper in half and round on outside corner.

   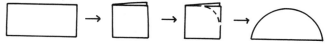

   Draw the ice blocks with crayon.

2. Round all four corners on the white and the light brown squares.

   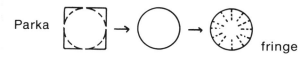

   Draw the face with crayon.

   Paste the face to the parka.

   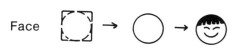

3. Fold the red mitten paper in half and cut on the fold. Round the top corners on both pieces.

   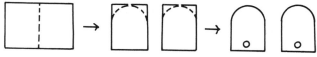

   Punch a hole for the yarn.

   Insert the yarn through the holes and knot.

4. Paste the yarn strip between the parka and the igloo.

   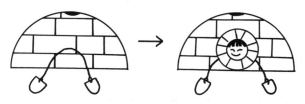

F f

Read it!

1. *The ABC Bunny* by Wanda Gag
2. *No Ducks In Our Bathtub* by Martha Alexander
3. *What Makes A Bird A Bird?* by May Garelick

Eat it!
Fortune Cookies

2 large eggs
½ cup sugar
4 Tbs. vegetable oil
½ cup cornstarch
2 Tbs. water (Add a little more if the mixture is too thick.)

1. Beat eggs slightly, then add the sugar and beat until smooth.
2. Add oil and mix well.
3. Add a little of this mixture to the cornstarch. Stir until smooth. Add this to the rest of the mixture. Mix well.
4. Drop by teaspoon onto a hot griddle. Spread to a 3″ circle. Brown on both sides.
5. While the cookie is still warm, place a fortune on a slip of paper in the center of the cookie and fold.

a.    b.    c.

Draw it!

Direct students to fold a blank piece of paper into four sections. Draw on the chalkboard or use oral instructions to guide students to draw the following:

1. Make a fluffy blue feather.
2. Make a big feather and a small one.
3. Make a brown feather with a black tip.
4. Make a feather in a hat.

Oral language Experience:
   Students dictate a sentence or short story about one of the pictures to an adult.

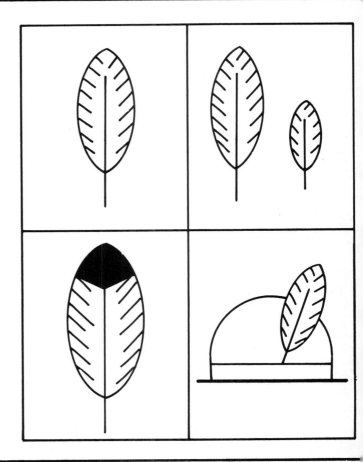

FUN WITH THE ALPHABET

Make it!   Funny, Fat Frog

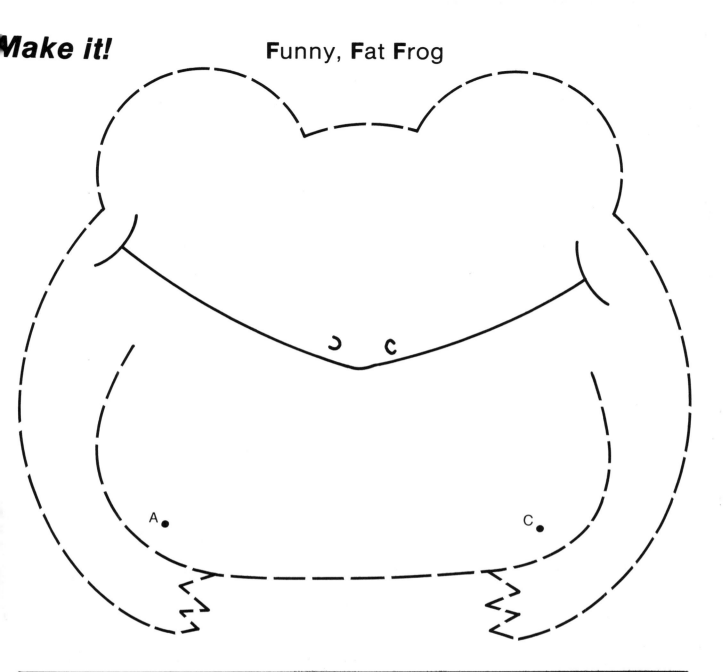

Materials:

- Reproduce the patterns on this and the following page on green construction paper.

- Paper fasteners

- Scissors, paste, crayons

- Construction paper:
  2- 1½" white squares
  2- 1" black squares

- Optional: thin strips of red paper for tongues

Bulletin Board Idea:

Start with a blue background.

Draw the water line with marking pen.

Cut out large green lily pads and staple to the board.

Put frogs on the lilypads , in the water, etc .

Steps to follow

1. Cut out the body and all 4 leg parts. When cutting the body, be sure to cut out the arms too.

2. Use paper fastener to attach the legs to the body. Attach A to A, B to B, etc. The feet sections may be turned over so that the toes point in or out.

3. To make the eyes:
   Round the black and white squares into circles.

   Paste the white circles to the frog.

   Paste the black circles inside the white circles.

4. Use a black crayon to trace the mouth and nose.

   A thin strip of red paper makes a nice tongue.

   Arms can be bent up.

Frog
Legs Pattern

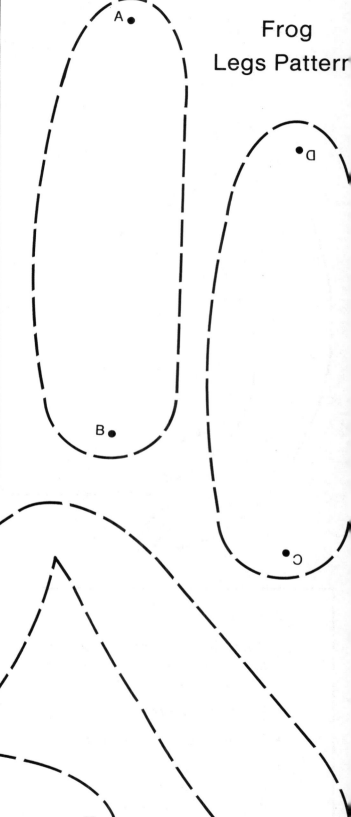

FUN WITH THE ALPHABET

Gg

Read it!

1. *The Guinea Pig ABC* by Kate Duke
2. *Little Gorilla* by Ruth Bornstein

Eat it!

"Garden Soup"

½ cup consomme
½ cup tomato juice
½ cup each chopped cucumber,
   tomato, green pepper
¼ cup chopped onion (optional)
1 Tbs. vegetable oil
½ tsp. salt

1. Mix all ingredients.
2. Chill and serve.
Serves 4-6

Serve graham crackers and grapes to less daring students.

Draw it!

Direct students to fold a blank piece of paper into four sections. Draw on the chalkboard or use oral instructions to guide students to draw the following:

1. Make a surprise gift with a red bow.

2. Make a big gift with a blue bow.

3. Make a gift with pretty polka dots.

4. Make a surprise gift. Make it colorful.

Oral language Experience:
  Students dictate a sentence or short story about one of the pictures to an adult.

Make it!   Great Grinning Gorilla

Materials:	Steps to follow:
• Reproduce this and the following page on white construction paper. • 2 paper fasteners • Scissors and crayons	1. Color the patterns. 2. Cut out the pieces. 3. Attach the gorilla's arms with paper fasteners.

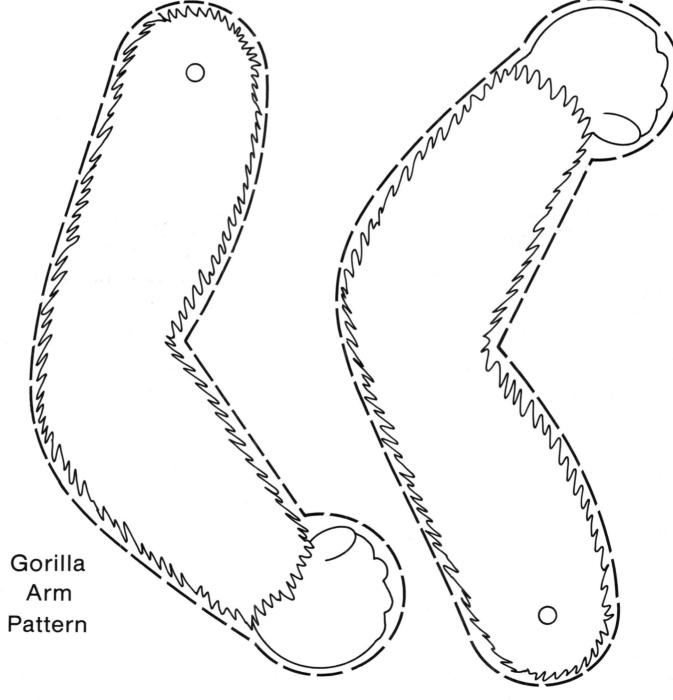

Gorilla
Arm
Pattern

         FUN WITH THE ALPHABET

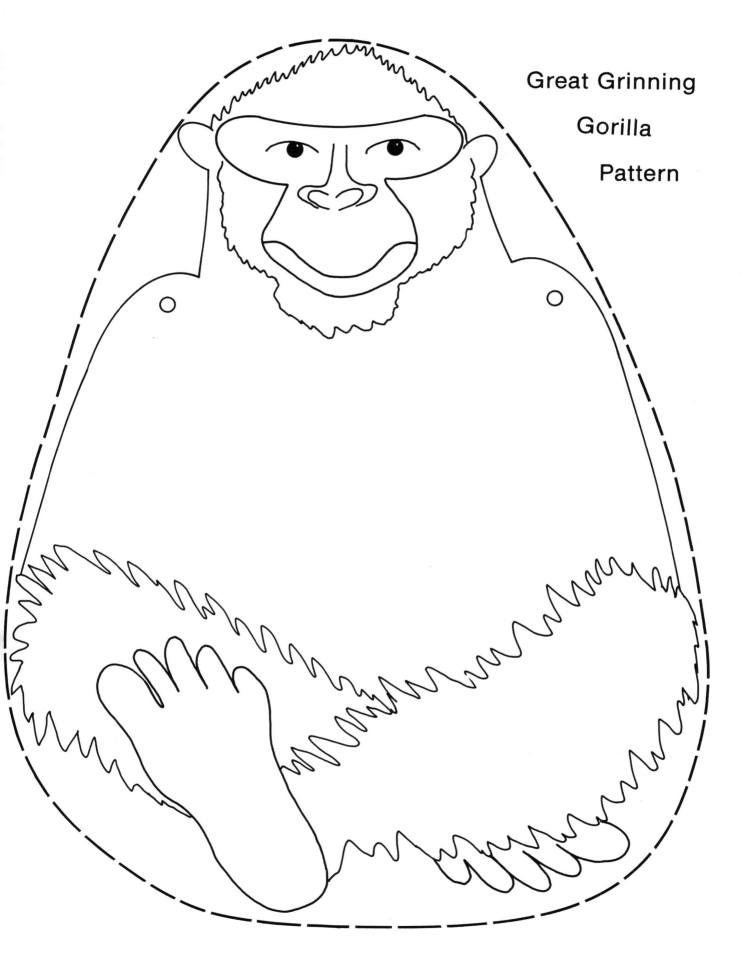

Great Grinning
Gorilla
Pattern

17

FUN WITH THE ALPHABET

Hh

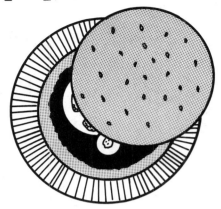

Read it!

1. *Helen Oxenburg's ABC of things* by Helen Oxenburg
2. *Lily At The Table* by Linda Heller
3. *The Little White House* by Virginia Lee Burton

Eat it!

"Hot Rod" Hot Dog

Hot dog
4 round pieces of zucchini or carrot for wheels
4 raisins for hubcaps
2 toothpicks

Taste honeycomb as an extra "h" treat.

Draw it!

Direct students to fold a blank piece of paper into four sections. Draw on the chalkboard or use oral instructions to guide students to draw the following:

1. Make a high green hill.
2. Make a little house on a hill.
3. Make a big house on a hill.
4. Make a house on a hill on a hazy (gray) day.

Oral language Experience:
   Students dictate a sentence or short story about one of the pictures to an adult.

Make it!

A **H**ealthy, **H**earty **H**amburger

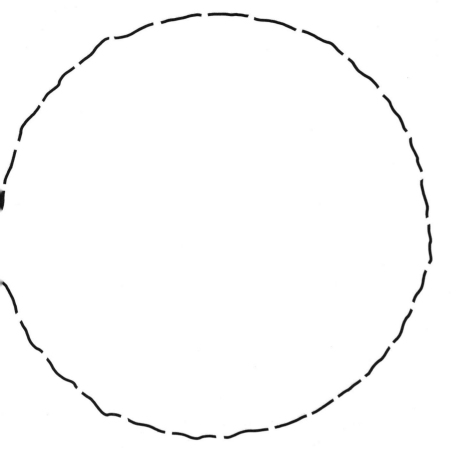

Color the meat patty brown.

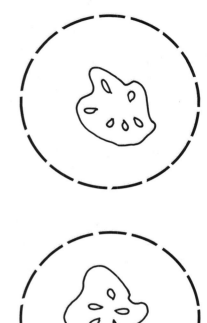

Color the pickles green.

Color the tomato red.

Materials:

- Reproduce this page on white construction paper.
- Reproduce the following page on light brown construction paper.
- Crayons, scissors, and paste
- Construction paper:

  3" square of yellow or orange for cheese
- Scraps of green for lettuce and white for onions
- Paper plates

     FUN WITH THE ALPHABET

Hamburger Bun Pattern

Steps to follow:

1.

Give each child a paper plate.

2.

Color and cut out all the parts.

3.

Paste the bottom bun on a paper plate.

Fold—put paste underneath.

4.

Assemble the hamburger pasting on the parts the child wishes to have on his/her hamburger.

Add mustard and catsup using crayons to color the bun.

Cheese can be a square yellow or orange.

Add scraps of green and white for lettuce and onion.

5.

Fold the top bun on the fold line. Put paste on the fold only, so the bun can be lifted to peek inside the hamburger.

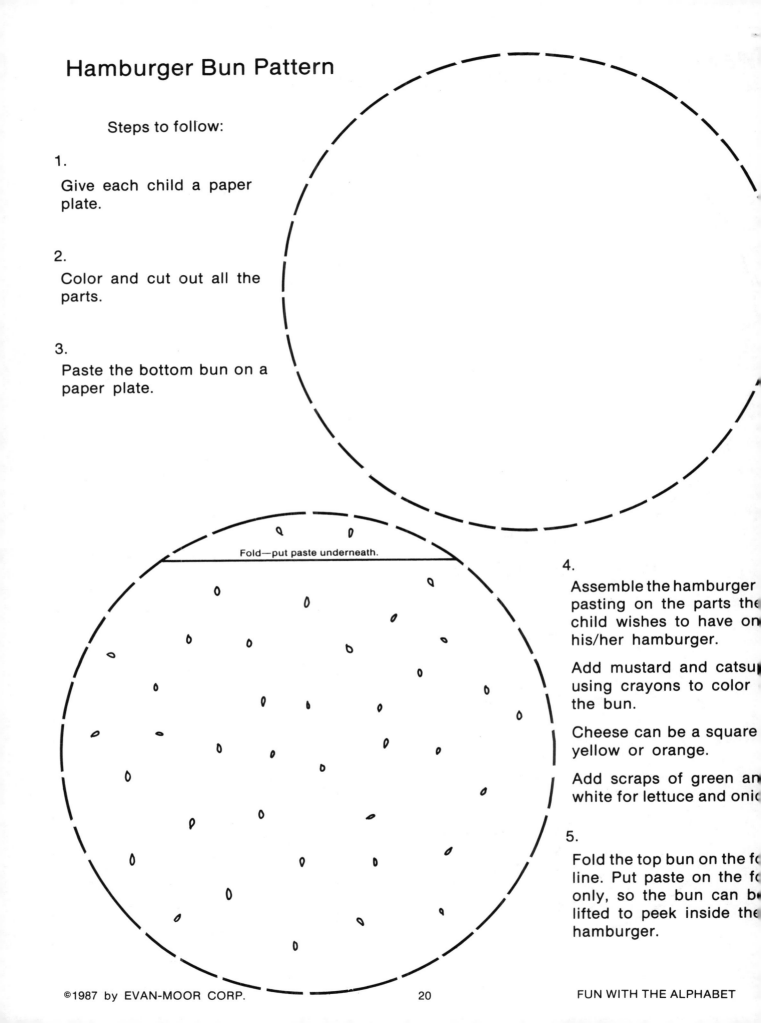

FUN WITH THE ALPHABET

I i

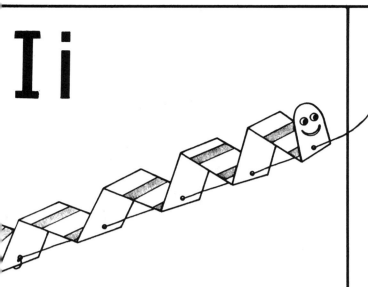

Read it!

1. *What's Inside? The Alphabet Book* by Satoshi Kitamura
2. *Eskimos* by Derek Fordham (shows how an igloo is made)
3. *Inch By Inch* by Leo Leonni

Eat it!

"Icky Stickys"

¼ cup margarine
4 cups miniature marshmallows
5 cups Rice Krispies
Ice cream sticks

1. Melt the margarine over low heat.
2. Add marshmallows. Stir until they melt. Then cook 3-4 mins. longer, stirring constantly.
3. Remove from the burner and add the cereal. Stir until the cereal is coated.
4. Form into balls and add an ice cream handle.

**This is very hot. An adult should form the balls. Butter your hands first!

Draw it!

Direct students to fold a blank piece of paper into four sections. Draw on the chalkboard or use oral instructions to guide students to draw the following:

1. Make an igloo made of ice.
2. Make an igloo with a fire inside.
3. Make a small igloo.
4. Make an igloo on a sunny day.

Oral language Experience:
   Students dictate a sentence or short story about one of the pictures to an adult.

Make it!

It's An Inch-along Inchworm

Inch this little worm across the floor by pulling the string.

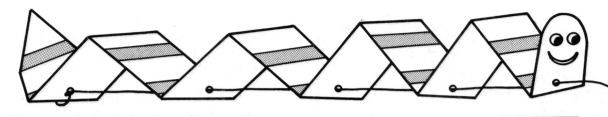

Materials:

- Bright colors of construction paper 2- 3" x 18" pasted together.
- 60" strip of yarn
- Hole punch
- Crayons, scissors
- Paper scraps

Steps to follow:

1. Paste the two strips of construction paper together.

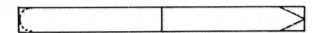

2. Round the corners on one end. Cut the other end to a point.

3. Accordion fold the strip. Teacher should mark the first segment at 3" to serve as a guide.

4. Pinch the segments together and punch one hole through the worm. The teacher should do this for the children.

5. Slip the yarn through the hole.

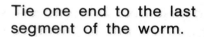

Tie one end to the last segment of the worm.

Tie a loop in the other end.

6. Use paper scraps or crayons to add details.

eyes

mouth

stripes

FUN WITH THE ALPHABET

Jj

Read it!

1. *Mouse Numbers And Letters* by Jim Arnosky
2. *Airport* by Byron Barton
3. *Jellyfish And Other Sea Creatures* by Oxford Scientific Films

Eat it!

"Jiggly" Jello and Juice

It's fun to make your gelatin in three colors (red, yellow, blue*) and practice color mixing. Children can then eat a rainbow of colors.

*Use unflavored gelatin with peppermint extract and blue food coloring.

Draw it!

Direct students to fold a blank piece of paper into four sections. Draw on the chalkboard or use oral instructions to guide students to draw the following:

1. Make a red jellyfish.
2. Make a green jellyfish with red tentacles.
3. Make two jellyfish. One is red and one is green.
4. Make a surprise jellyfish.

Oral language Experience:
   Students dictate a sentence or short story about one of the pictures to an adult.

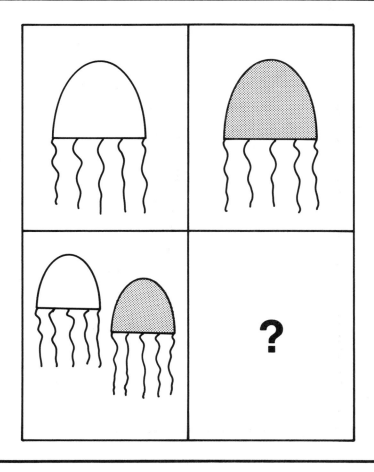

Make it!

Jiffy Jumbo Jet
Wings and Tail

Materials:

- Reproduce the patterns on this and the following page on white, gray, or light blue construction paper.
- Scissors
- Razor or mat knife
- Crayons

Steps to follow:

1. Cut out all the parts.

2. Decorate the jet parts with crayons. Add more windows, numbers, etc.

3. Assemble the jet by slipping wings and tail through proper precut slits. (An adult will need to cut these slits.)

4. To make the engines:

   a. Paste to form a cylinder.

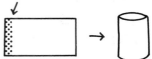

   b. Paste a cylinder on the underside of each wing.

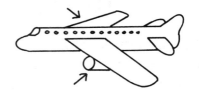

This jet is strictly kidpowered. It will not fly if thrown.

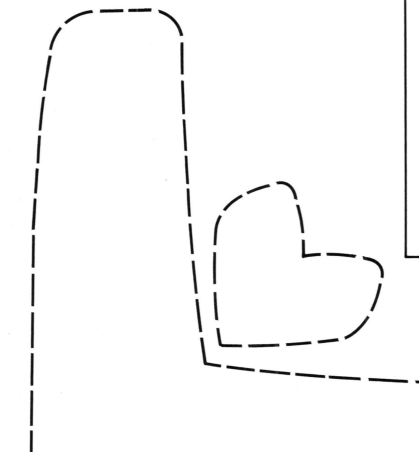

FUN WITH THE ALPHABET

Jiffy Jumbo Jet

Body and Engines

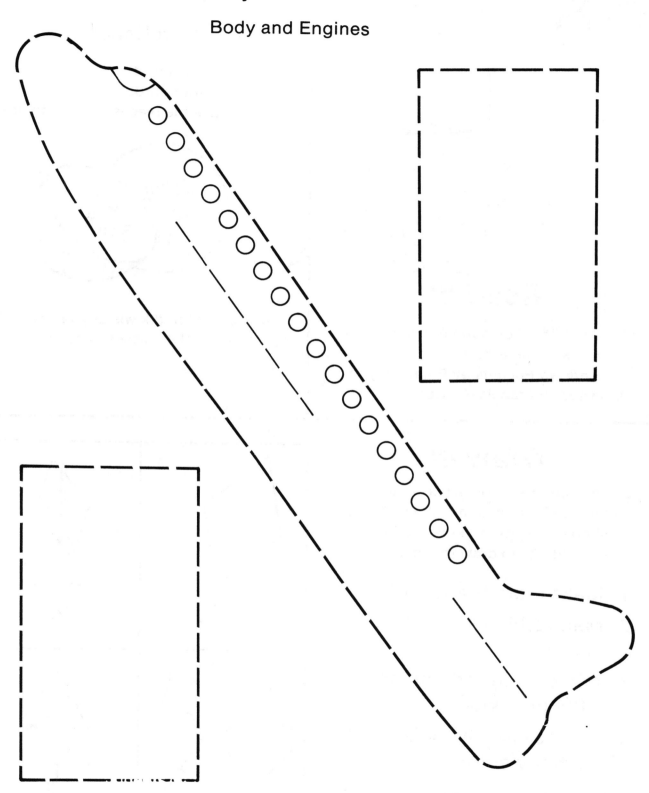

Hint: To save time when making the jet, cut the slits for the wing and tail with a razor blade or mat knife before you give the paper to the children to cut out.

                   FUN WITH THE ALPHABET

Kk

Read it!

1. *All In The Woodland Early, An ABC Book* by Jane Yolan
2. *Katy No Pockets* by Emmy Payne
3. *Kites* by Francis H. Wise

Eat it!

Kiwi Kabobs

1. Peel kiwi fruit.
2. Cut into thirds.
3. Place the pieces on a toothpick.

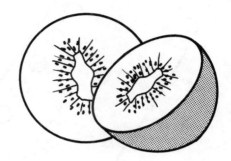

If you can't find kiwis at your market, have chocolate kisses instead.

Draw it!

Direct students to fold a blank piece of paper into four sections. Draw on the chalkboard or use oral instructions to guide students to draw the following:

1. Make a big orange kite.
2. Make a blue kite with a purple tail.
3. Make a big red kite and a little blue kite.
4. Make a kite with polka dots of many colors.

Oral language Experience:
   Students dictate a sentence or short story about one of the pictures to an adult.

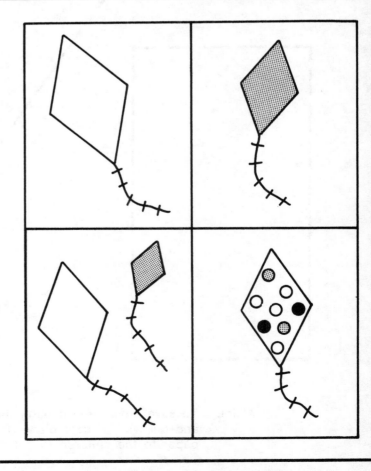

 FUN WITH THE ALPHABET

Make it!

Koko, the Kicking Kangaroo

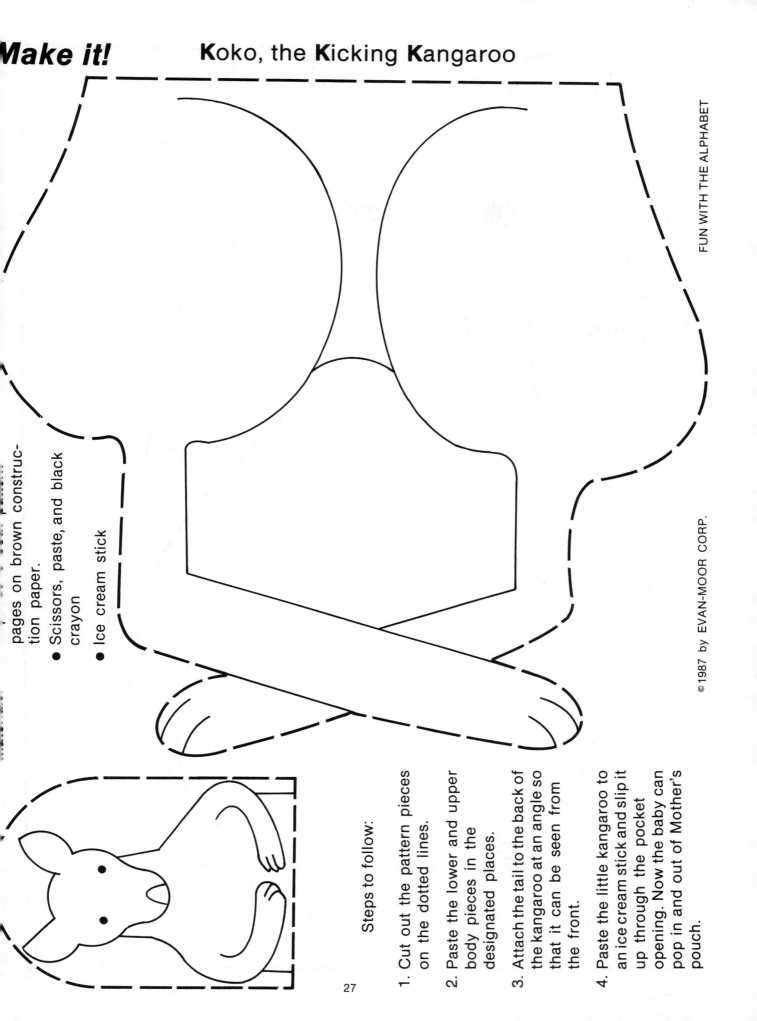

©1987 by EVAN-MOOR CORP.

pages on brown construction paper.

• Scissors, paste, and black crayon

• Ice cream stick

Steps to follow:

1. Cut out the pattern pieces on the dotted lines.

2. Paste the lower and upper body pieces in the designated places.

3. Attach the tail to the back of the kangaroo at an angle so that it can be seen from the front.

4. Paste the little kangaroo to an ice cream stick and slip it up through the pocket opening. Now the baby can pop in and out of Mother's pouch.

27

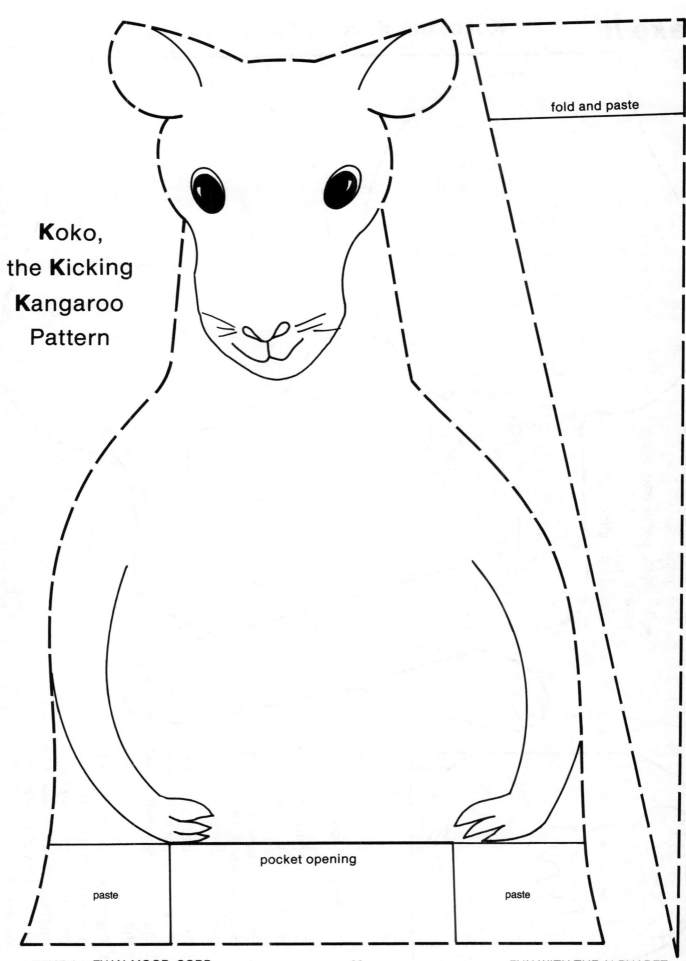

Koko,
the **K**icking
Kangaroo
Pattern

fold and paste

pocket opening

paste

paste

28 FUN WITH THE ALPHABET

Ll

Read it!

1. *My Name Is Alice* by Jane Bayer
2. *Lambs For Dinner* by Betsy and Giulio Maestro
3. *circles, triangles and squares* by Tana Hoban

Eat it!

Lemonade and Ladyfingers

Make lemonade:
1. Squeeze the juice of ½ a lemon into a glass with ½ cup water.
2. Sweeten to taste. Add ice cubes.
Or...use frozen lemonade concentrate.
Buy ladyfingers at your favorite bakery or supermarket.

Draw it!

Direct students to fold a blank piece of paper into four sections. Draw on the chalkboard or use oral instructions to guide students to draw the following:

1. Make a sweet orange lollipop.
2. Make a big grape lollipop.
3. Make two lemon lollipops.
4. Make a lollipop with a twirl.

Oral language Experience:
   Students dictate a sentence or short story about one of the pictures to an adult.

Make it!

Lovely Little Lamb

This little lamb can have curly paper wool or fuzzy cotton wool. Curly or fuzzy, he's sure to be a favorite.

Materials:

- White or gray construction paper:

  1- 6" x 9" for body
  1- 4" x 6" for head

- Black construction paper:

  2- 2" x 4½" for legs
  1- 3" x 5" for ear
  2- ¾" squares for eye and nose

- 10 or 12- 2" squares of white ditto paper to cut into spirals OR...cotton balls.

- Black crayon, scissors, paste

- Optional: Reproduce the "spiral" patterns on the following page.

Steps to follow:

1. Round off the corners of the two large white (or gray) papers to form the head and body. Save a corner scrap for a tail.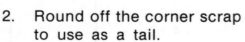

2. Round off the corner scrap to use as a tail.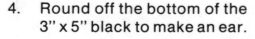

3. Paste the head and tail in place.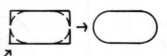

4. Round off the bottom of the 3" x 5" black to make an ear.

5. Paste the ear on the head and paste the two 2" x 4½" black on the body for legs.

6. Round the two ¾" black squares into circles for the eye and nose. Paste the eye and nose in place and use the black crayon to add a mouth.

7. Add the fleece:

   Cut the 2" white squares into circles, then into spirals. OR...use the spiral patterns on the following page. Paste one end of the spiral onto the lamb so the curl will stick out. Cover the body with curls and put one on the lamb's forehead.

   OR...use cotton to cover the body and the forehead. Have the children spread the cotton balls out before pasting.

   Hint: If you use cottonballs, have the paste put on the paper. Then lay the cotton on the paste.

FUN WITH THE ALPHABET

Lamb Fleece Pattern Spirals

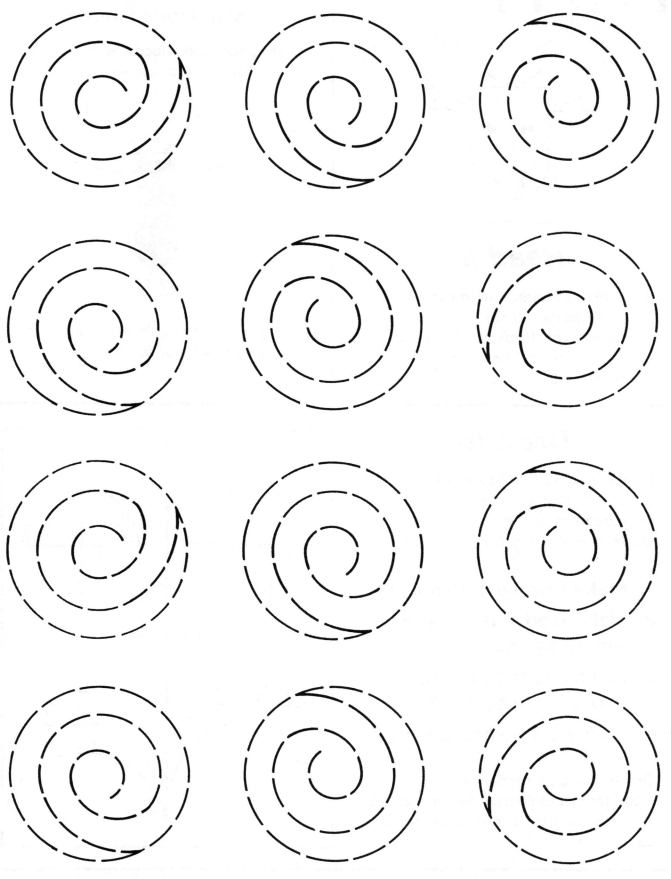

31   FUN WITH THE ALPHABET

Mm

Read it!

1. *A Merry Mouse Christmas ABC*
   by Priscilla Hillmar
2. *Morris The Moose* by B. Wiseman
3. *Mushroom In The Rain*
   by Mirra Ginsburg

Eat it!

Marvelous Mousse

Use packaged chocolate mousse or
your favorite mousse recipe.

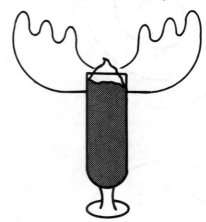

Share your chocolate mousse with
your puppet moose.

Draw it!

Direct students to fold a blank piece of
paper into four sections. Draw on the
chalkboard or use oral instructions to
guide students to draw the following:

1. Make a brown mushroom.
2. Make a red mushroom with
   yellow spots.
3. Make two brown mush-
   rooms on a brown hill.
4. Make a surprise mushroom.

Oral language Experience:
   Students dictate a sentence or short
story about one of the pictures to an
adult.

Make it!

Marvelous Mighty Moose
A Bag Puppet

What "m" foods could this hungry moose have for lunch?

Materials:

- One brown lunch bag

- Light brown construction paper: Head 9" x 5"
  Ears 2- 4 ½" x 2"

- Red construction paper for a tongue: 3" x 6"

- Reproduce the antler pattern on the following page on dark brown construction paper.

- Black paper scraps

- Scissors, crayons

Steps to follow:

1. Round two corners on the large brown paper.

   Paste this piece to the paper bag.

2. Trace around the moose's nose with brown crayon to create the jaw line on the bag.

   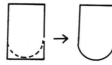

3. Round two corners on the red tongue paper.

   Paste the tongue under the bag flap.

   Draw teeth along the jaw line.

   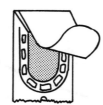

4. Cut out the antler pattern. Paste the antlers to the back of the bag.

5. Round two corners on the ear pieces.

   Paste the ears behind the antlers.

6. Cut a black circle for eyes and then cut in half.

   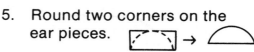

   Cut two black ovals for nostrils.

   Paste the eyes and nostrils to the moose's nose.

FUN WITH THE ALPHABET

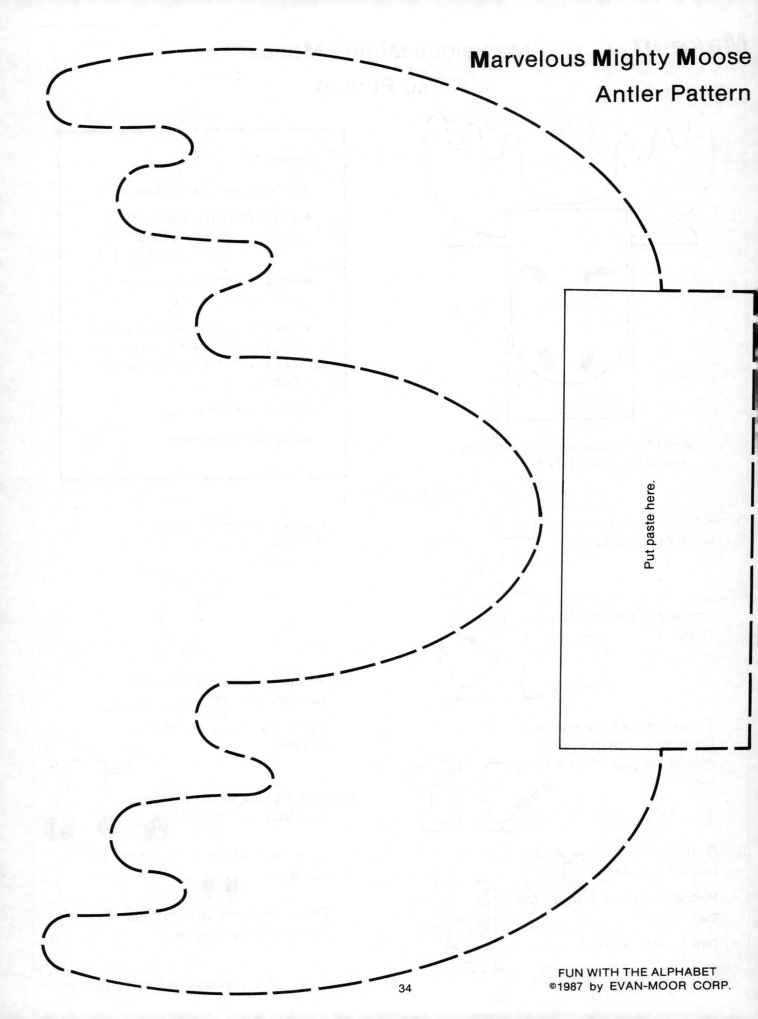

Put paste here.

34

Nn

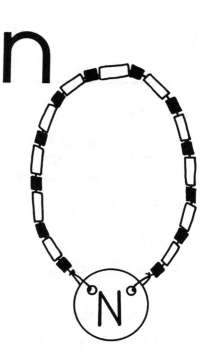

Read it!

1. *Alligators All Around, An Alphabet* by Maurice Sendak
2. *The Best Nest* by P. D. Eastman

Eat it!

Nuts and Nibbles

1 package Wheat Chex and Rice Chex
1 package of Cheerios
1 package thin pretzel sticks
1 lb. salted nuts
¼ lb. margarine ⎫
½ lb. butter   ⎬ melted
1 tsp. Worchestershire Sauce
½ tsp. garlic salt

1. Mix all ingredients in roasting pan.
2. Bake $200°$ for 2 hours. Stir occasionally.

Draw it!

Direct students to fold a blank piece of paper into four sections. Draw on the chalkboard or use oral instructions to guide students to draw the following:

1. Make a brown nest.

2. Make a white egg in a brown nest.

3. Make a crack in an egg in a brown nest.

4. Make a surprise in a brown nest.

Oral language Experience:
   Students dictate a sentence or short story about one of the pictures to an adult.

FUN WITH THE ALPHABET

Make it!

Nifty Noodle Necklace

It's always fun to wear jewelry you've made all by yourself!

Materials:

- Various sizes and styles of noodles. Choose those that can be easily strung.
- Rubbing alcohol and food coloring. Choose 3 bright colors.
- Approximately 1 yard of heavy string
- Masking tape
- Tagboard shapes for medallions
- White glue and glitter for lettering the medallions
- Hole punch
- Quart jar with lid

Steps to follow:

1. Dye the noodles.

   a. Put ½" rubbing alcohol and 20 or more drops of food coloring in a quart jar. (Experiment to find the shade you like best.)

   b. Fill 2/3 full of noodles. Shake well. Spread the noodles on waxed paper to dry.

2. Punch 2 holes in the medallion.

   Tie one end of the string to the medallion.

   Wrap masking tape around the other end of the string to make a "needle".

3. String the noodles. This is a good time to practice patterning. Let each child choose a pattern to follow. Lay an example in front of the child to refer to while stringing.

4. When the necklace is the desired length, tie the open end to the other hole on the medallion. Cut off the excess string.

5. Write the child's initials on the medallion with white glue. The child can sprinkle on glitter. Let it dry thoroughly!

   Now it is ready to wear.

Read it!

1. *Handtalk, An ABC of Finger Spelling And Sign Language* by Remy Charlip, Mary Beth and George Ancona
2. *Otter In The Cave* by Miska Miles
3. *The Random House Book of Poetry for Children* selected by Jack Prelutsky has a whole section of "food" poems!

Eat it!

Olive Tasting Time!

Try black olives, green olives, and for brave little children...olives with pimento!

Draw it!

Direct students to fold a blank piece of paper into four sections. Draw on the chalkboard or use oral instructions to guide students to draw the following:

1. Make an oval green olive.
2. Make an oval green olive with red pimiento.
3. Make a black olive with a hole in it.
4. Make a green olive and a black olive.

Oral language Experience:
   Students dictate a sentence or short story about one of the pictures to an adult.

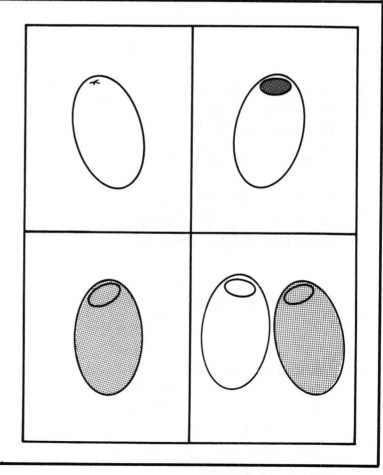

Make it!

Oliver, the Sea Otter

This little sea otter is enjoying his lunch.

Steps to follow:

1. Round one end of the 6" x 18" body, the 2- 3" x 5" front paws and the 2" x 12" tail.

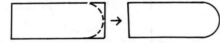

2. Cut a slit approximately 5" up from the bottom on the body to form the hind legs.

    Fold the feet up.

3. Paste the front paws on the back of the body, leaving about 5" for the head.

    Paste the tail on the back of the body above the leg slit.

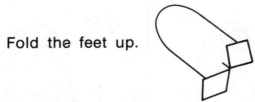

4. To make the otter's face:

    Round the 1½" x 2" piece of black into an oval nose.

    Round the 1" black squares into circular eyes.

    Paste the eyes, nose, and whiskers on the otter's face. Tape will help to hold the whiskers in place.

5. Optional:
    Cut a shell and a rock from gray, white, or light brown construction paper, or use a pebble and a real shell.

    Paste the rock on the otter's chest. Paste the shell on the otter's front paw. Bend the paw so the otter can "pound" the shell on the rock to break it open.

Pp

Read it!

1. *A is for Aloha* by Stephanie Feeney
2. *Pigs In Hiding*
   by Arlene Dubanivich
3. *The Popcorn Book*
   by Tomie de Paola

Eat it!

Pickle Party

Taste all types of pickles. Be sure to include watermelon pickles and pickled pigs' feet!

If your group isn't too adventurous, have a popcorn party instead.

Draw it!

Direct students to fold a blank piece of paper into four sections. Draw on the chalkboard or use oral instructions to guide students to draw the following:

1. Make a piece of popcorn popping out of a pan.

2. Make two pieces of popcorn popping out of a pan.

3. Make lots of popcorn popping out of a pan.

4. Make a popcorn ball out of all the popcorn.

Oral language Experience:
    Students dictate a sentence or short story about one of the pictures to an adult.

Make it!

Perky Pink Pig

This charming pig is fun to make. It can be easily turned into a puppet by pasting it onto a tongue depressor. Now you are all set to act out The Three Little Pigs.

Materials:

- Pink construction paper:

  1- 7" square for head
  1- 4" square for snout
  1- 2½" square for ears
  1- 1½" x 3" strip

- Black crayon

- Scissors, paste

- Optional - tongue depressor

Steps to follow:

1. Round the 7" square and the 4" square for the head and the snout.

2. Color oval nostrils on the snout.

   Hint- Here is a good time to talk about the difference between an oval and a circle.

3. Make the 1½" x 3" strip into a cylinder by putting paste on the short side.

   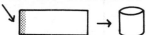

   Hint- Tell the children to hold the cylinder closed while they (or you) count to 10. This will give the paste time to set.

4. Paste the snout on one side of the cylinder and paste the other side of the cylinder to the pig's face.

   This will make the snout stand out.

5. Cut the 2½" square from corner to corner to make ears.

   Hint- This is a good time to talk about diagonals.

6. Paste ears on the face. This can be done several ways.

7. Use crayon to draw on the eyes and a mouth.

   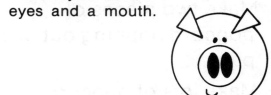

Optional: To turn your pig into a puppet, just paste it onto a tongue depressor.

Children who finish early may want to add a flower behind one ear or a hat on top, so have scraps of construction paper handy.

Qq

Read it!

1. *The Great Big Alphabet Picture Book With Lots of Words* by Richard Hefter and Martin Stephen Moskof
2. *Lemon Moon* by Kay Chorao
3. Read the "q" verse from *The ABC Bunny* by Wanda Gag

Eat it!

Quite Tasty Quilt

Children create pretty designs on crackers.

Use:

    cream cheese
    peanut butter
    "squeeze" cheese
        —on soda crackers

    frosting
        —on graham crackers

Add color with bits of vegetables, nuts, fruits or chocolate bits.

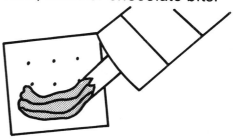

Draw it!

Direct students to fold a blank piece of paper into four sections. Draw on the chalkboard or use oral instructions to guide students to draw the following:

1. Make a quilt with red ends and a red circle.

2. Make a quilt. Divide it into quarters. Put a blue square in each quarter.

3. Make a quilt with lace around the edge.

4. Make a surprise quilt for a queen. Make it colorful.

Oral language Experience:
  Students dictate a sentence or short story about one of the pictures to an adult.

Make it!   Quick, Quiet Quail

Father Quail leads a covey
of babies out for their
morning search for food.

Materials:

> Reproduce the quail family
> pattern on white construction
> paper.
>
> Green construction paper
> 6" x 18"
>
> Scissors, crayons and paste

Steps to follow:

1. Color the quail brown.

2. Cut on the dotted lines.

3. Fold the flaps under and
   paste the quail to the
   green paper.

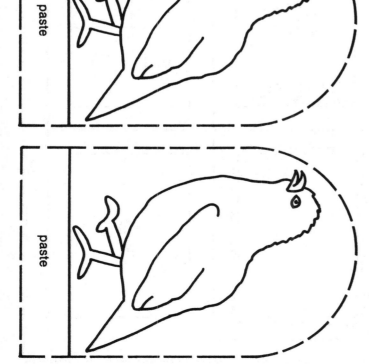

Rr

Read it!

1. *Apricot ABC* by Miska Miles
2. *Applebrum's Have A Robot* by Jane Thayer
3. *Little Raccoon* by Suzanne Noguere

Eat it!

Rice and Raisin Pudding

(8- ½ cup servings)

2 cups uncooked instant rice
3 cups milk
6 tbs. sugar
½ tsp. salt
½ tsp. cinnamon
½ cup seedless raisins

1. Combine all ingredients in a sauce pan.
2. Bring to a full rolling boil. Stir constantly.
3. Remove from heat and let stand 12—15 minutes, stirring occasionally. Serve warm or cool.

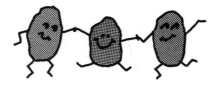

Draw it!

Direct students to fold a blank piece of paper into four sections. Draw on the chalkboard or use oral instructions to guide students to draw the following:

1. Make Rocky Robot. Color him red.

2. Make Roberta Robot. She is blue.

3. Make Ringo Robot orange.

4. Make poor Ray Robot. He stayed out in the rain. He is all rusty now.

Oral language Experience:
   Students dictate a sentence or short story about one of the pictures to an adult.

Make it!

Rowdy, the **R**ascal

Raccoon Mask

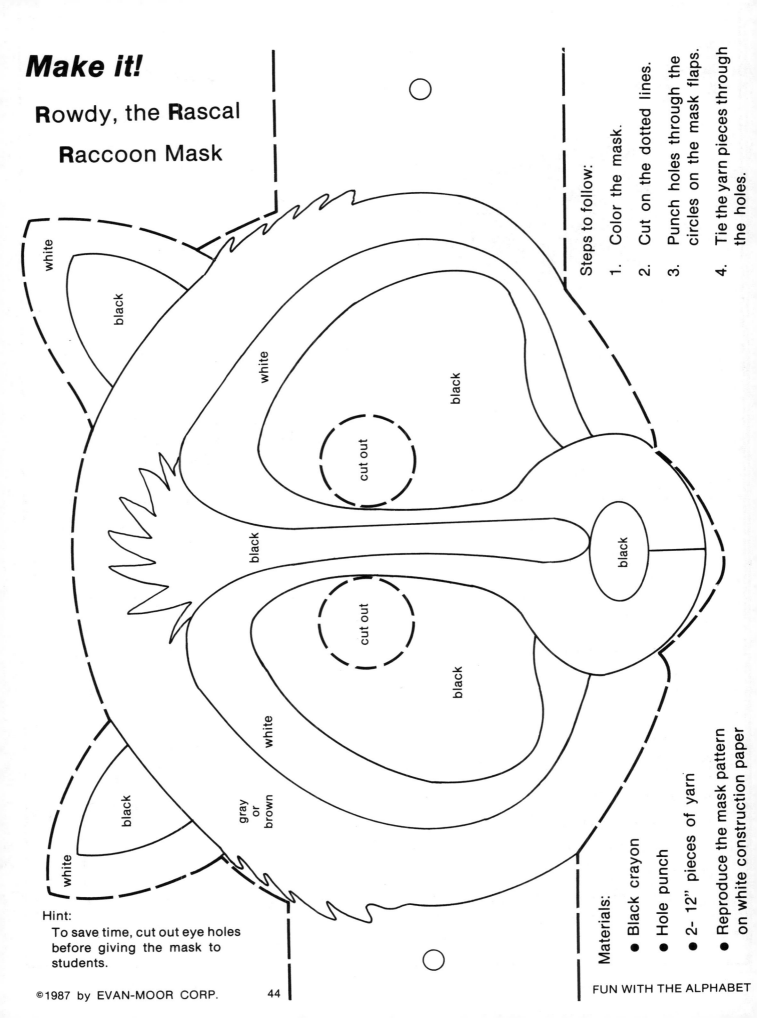

Steps to follow:

1. Color the mask.
2. Cut on the dotted lines.
3. Punch holes through the circles on the mask flaps.
4. Tie the yarn pieces through the holes.

white

black

white

black

black

black

cut out

cut out

black

white

black

gray or brown

white

black

white

Materials:
- Black crayon
- Hole punch
- 2- 12" pieces of yarn
- Reproduce the mask pattern on white construction paper

Hint:
To save time, cut out eye holes before giving the mask to students.

Ss

Read it!

1. *ABC, An Alphabet Book* by Thomas Matthiesen
2. *Ruby's Revenge* by Cheryl Pelavin
3. *Spiders* by Ramona Steward Dupre

Eat it!

"Sticky" Spaghetti

1. Cook the spaghetti in a small pan with less water than usual. *Overcook* the spaghetti.

2. Drain the spaghetti, but *don't* rinse it. Cool the spaghetti. (This much can be done at home if you prefer. Store in a plastic bag in the refrigerator until ready to use.)

3. Each child gets a portion to nibble on as he creates a picture on construction paper using one or two strands. They will not need glue. This is *really sticky* spaghetti!

Draw it!

Direct students to fold a blank piece of paper into four sections. Draw on the chalkboard or use oral instructions to guide students to draw the following:

1. Make a brown spider. He must have 8 legs.

2. Make a red spider on a green leaf.

3. Make a black spider hanging from his thread.

4. Make a green spider walking up a wall.

Oral language Experience:
   Students dictate a sentence or short story about one of the pictures to an adult.

Make it!

Sweet, Silly Skunk

These are the kind of "little stinkers" you like to have around.

Steps to follow:

Materials:

- Black construction paper:

  1- 9" x 12" for body
  1- 6" x 9" for tail
  1- 6" square for head
  2- 3" squares for ears

- Brown construction paper:

  1- 1" x 2" for nose
  2- 1" squares for eyes

- White construction paper:

  1- 3" x 4" for topknot
  2- 12" x 1½" for stripes

- Paper fastener

- Scissors, paste

1. Round the 9" x 12" black paper into an oval for the body.

   Round the 6" black square into a circle for the head.

   Round the two 3" black squares into circles for ears.

2. Paste one of the 1½" white strips near the top of the large body oval to make the skunk's stripes.

   Trim off the extra.

3. Paste the head, and body together.

   Paste the ears on the back of the head.

   The head covers part of the stripes.

4. Make a topknot out of the 3" x 4" white paper. Cut irregular-shaped triangles out of the edges of the paper, cutting into the center.

   Paste the topknot on the skunk's forehead.

5. Round the brown pieces to form an oval nose and 2 circle eyes. Paste on the face.

6. Making the tail:

   Round the top two corners on the 6" x 9" black paper.

   Paste a white strip across the tail. Trim off excess.

   Attach the tail to the body of the skunk.

7. Use white crayon to draw the mouth, front feet, and hind leg.

Tt

Read it!

1. *I Unpacked My Grandmother's Trunk* by Susan Ramsey Hoguet
2. Read the poem "Eletelephony" by Laura E. Richards
3. Read the poem "The Toaster" by William Jay Smith

Eat it!

Toast and Tasty Toppings

Toast your favorite kind of bread.

Top with:

Butter and jam
Peanut butter and banana rounds
Cream cheese and sweet pickles

Draw it!

Direct students to fold a blank piece of paper into four sectons. Draw on the chalkboard or use oral instructions to guide students to draw the following:

1. Make toast with butter.

2. Make toast with cheese.

3. Make toast with jam. A bite is missing.

4. Make burnt toast.

Oral language Experience:
   Students dictate a sentence or short story about one of the pictures to an adult.

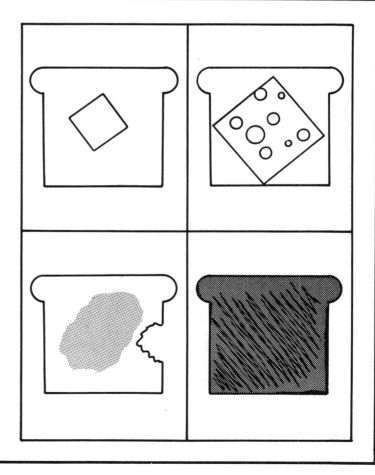

Make it!   Telephone Talk

This lesson is a fine way to offer practice in learning your own phone number.

Materials:

- Reproduce the patterns on this and the following page on construction paper.
- Scissors, crayons, paste
- Hole punch
- 20" of yarn for the connecting cord
- Paper fastener
- 2 paperclips

Steps to follow:

1. Color and cut out the telephone parts.

2. Attach the dial. Use a paper fastener for the round dial or paste on the "push button" dial.

3. An adult will need to punch holes in the receiver and the base. Tie the yarn strip through the holes.

4. Cut slits on the telephone and insert paper clips to hold the receiver.

Use the type of dial you have on your phone at home.

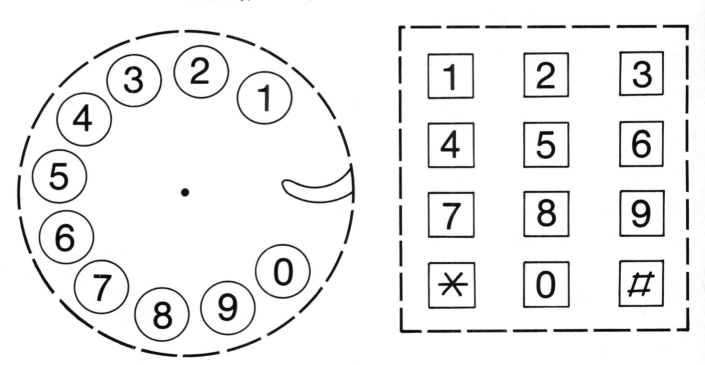

Display Hint: Pin all the students' phones to a bulletin board.

Use the phones to the practice phone manners and emergency procedures.

Pattern for **T**elephone **T**alk

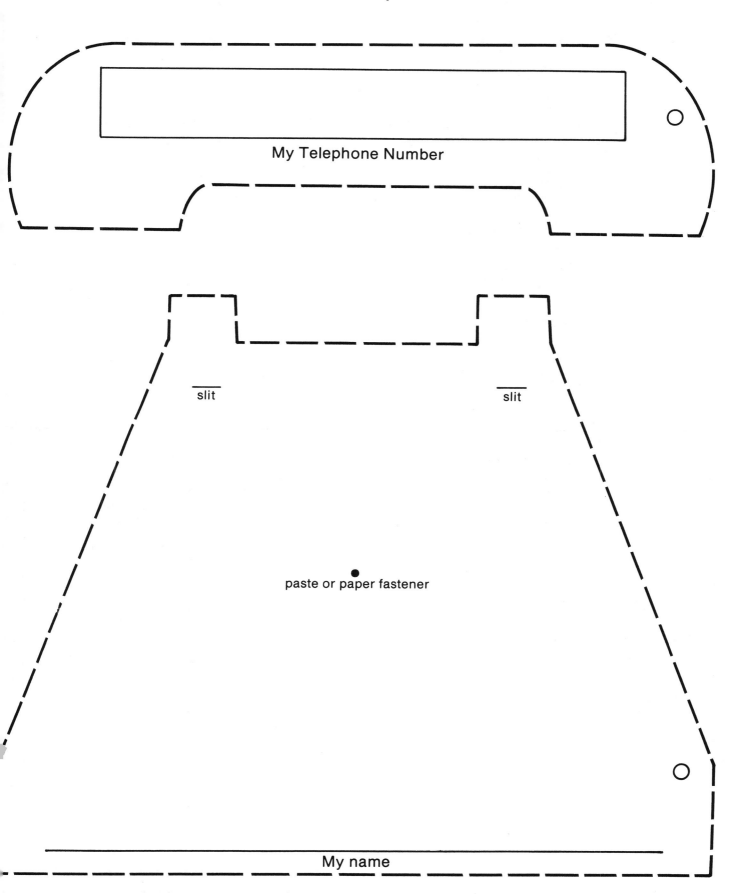

My Telephone Number

slit   slit

•
paste or paper fastener

My name

         FUN WITH THE ALPHABET

Uu

Read it!

1. *ABC Say With Me* by Karen Gundersheimer
2. *Umbrella* by Taro Yashima

Eat it!

"Unusual" Snacks

1. Spinach and peanut butter roll-ups
2. Rutabaga and turnip circles
3. Sardines and crackers
4. Rice crackers and applebutter

Let your students think up other "unusual" snacks to try.

Draw it!

Direct students to fold a blank piece of paper into four sections. Draw on the chalkboard or use oral instructions to guide students to draw the following:

1. Make a red umbrella.
2. Make a yellow umbrella with purple polka dots.
3. Make a green umbrella in the rain.
4. Make an upside down orange umbrella.

Oral language Experience:
   Students dictate a sentence or short story about one of the pictures to an adult.

Make it!

Umpire

This umpire is ready to make any call. Three strikes and you're out!

Materials:

- Black construction paper:
  1-4½" x 12" for body
  1-2½" x 4½" for hat
  2-2" x 6" for arms
  2-½" x 5" for bars on mask
- Flesh construction paper
  1-4½" x 6" for face
  2-1½" x 1½" for hands
- Paper egg carton bottom cut in half
- Paste, scissors, and crayons
- 2 paper fasteners

Steps to follow:

1. Fold the black body paper in half. Cut up the center of the lower half.

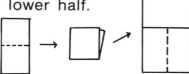

2. Paste the egg carton to the main body part.

   Fold the paper at the knees.

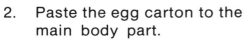
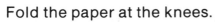

3. Paste the face paper behind the body paper. Overlap 2 inches.

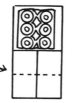

4. Fold the hat paper in half.

   Paste the hat to the top of the face so brim sticks out.

   Round the top corners of the hat and head.

5. Draw the face with crayon.

6. Paste the two protective face mask bars over the face. Paste only the ends so that the center forms an arch.

7. Round the top edges of the black arms.

   Round the corners on the flesh hands.

   Paste the hands to the arms. Attach the arms at the shoulder with paper fasteners.

51   FUN WITH THE ALPHABET

Vv

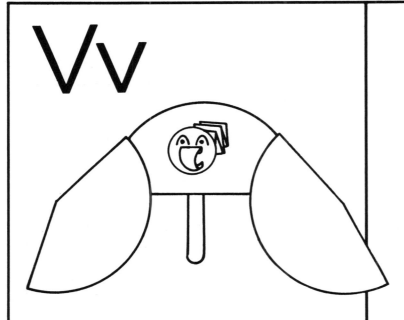

Read it!

1. *Victoria's ABC Adventure* by Cathy Warren
2. *Eli* by Bill Peet
3. *Vans* by Judi R. Kesselman and Franklynn Peterson

Eat it!

Very Vegetable Soup

4 quarts chicken or beef broth
1 chopped onion (optional)
2 cups sliced carrots
2 cups sliced celery
2 cans tomatoes
2 cups cubed potato
1 pkg. frozen corn
pepper and salt to taste
1 bay leaf

1. Put all ingredients in a soup pot.
2. Simmer until "veggies" are tender.
3. Remove bay leaf before serving.

Draw it!

Direct students to fold a blank piece of paper into four sections. Draw on the chalkboard or use oral instructions to guide students to draw the following:

1. Make an orange van on the road.

2. Make a red van on the grass.

3. Make a green van going down hill.

4. Make a blue van going uphill.

Oral language Experience:
   Students dictate a sentence or short story about one of the pictures to an adult.

Make it! Very Valuable Vulture

This turkey vulture is ready to perch on your desk or a friend's shoulder.

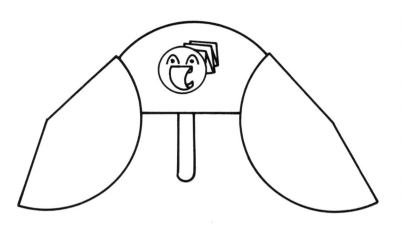

Materials:

- Black construction paper
  3- 9" x 6" for body and wings

- Red construction paper
  1- 2" x 5" for neck
  1- 3" x 3" for head

- Yellow construction paper
  1- 2" x 2" for beak

- Tongue depressor

- Cellophane tape

- Paste, crayons, scissors

Steps to follow:

1. Make the body:

   Round the top corners on the 3 black rectangles to form the body and wings.

   Paste these three pieces together in a line.

   Bend the side flaps down.

   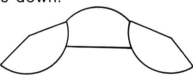

2. Make the head:

   Round the corners on the red square to form the head

   Cut the yellow square to make a beak.

   Curl the tip of the beak on a pencil. Fold down the base.

   Paste the beak to the head.

   Add eyes with a black crayon.

   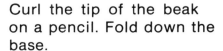
   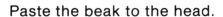

3. Make the neck:

   Accordian fold the red 2" x 5" to make the neck.

   Paste one end of this strip to the main body piece. Then paste the other end to the head. Now the head has a 3-D quality.

4. Attach a tongue depressor handle to the back of the main body piece with the cellophane tape.

53   FUN WITH THE ALPHABET

Ww

Read it!

1. *The Animal Picture Word Book* by Claudia Zeff

Note: The ABC portion is at the back. The pictures are wonderful for vocabulary development and visual perception.

2. *Walpole* by Syd Hoff
3. *The Box With Red Wheels* by Maud and Miska Petersham

Eat it!

Wonderful Waffles

Use frozen waffles or make up your favorite recipe.
Top with syrup and butter or whipped cream and fresh fruit.

Draw it!

Direct students to fold a blank piece of paper into four sections. Draw on the chalkboard or use oral instructions to guide students to draw the following:

1. Make a red wagon on the grass.
2. Make a red wagon rolling downhill.
3. Make a green ball in a purple wagon.
4. Make a surprise wagon. Make it colorful.

Oral language Experience:
   Students dictate a sentence or short story about one of the pictures to an adult.

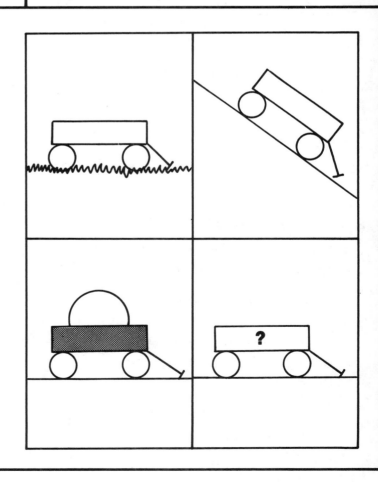

Make it!

Willy, the **W**iggly **W**alrus

This walrus is swimming in the icy waters looking for his lunch.

Materials:

- Blue construction paper for the background sheet 9" x 12"
- Reproduce the walrus pattern on the following page on white construction paper.
- A drinking straw
- Crayons, scissors, and paste
- Razor blade or mat knife
- Stapler

Steps to follow:

1. Fold up about 3" on the bottom of the blue paper.

2. Make a 1" slit in the fold line.

   Cut a wave line along the bottom.

3. Staple the flap up.

4. Cut out the ice floe from the pattern page and paste to the blue paper.

5. Color the walrus brown and cut out on the dotted line.

   Tape the straw to the back.

   Slip the straw through the slit in the fold line of the blue paper.

6. Color the fish. Cut them out and paste in the water.

Walrus Pattern

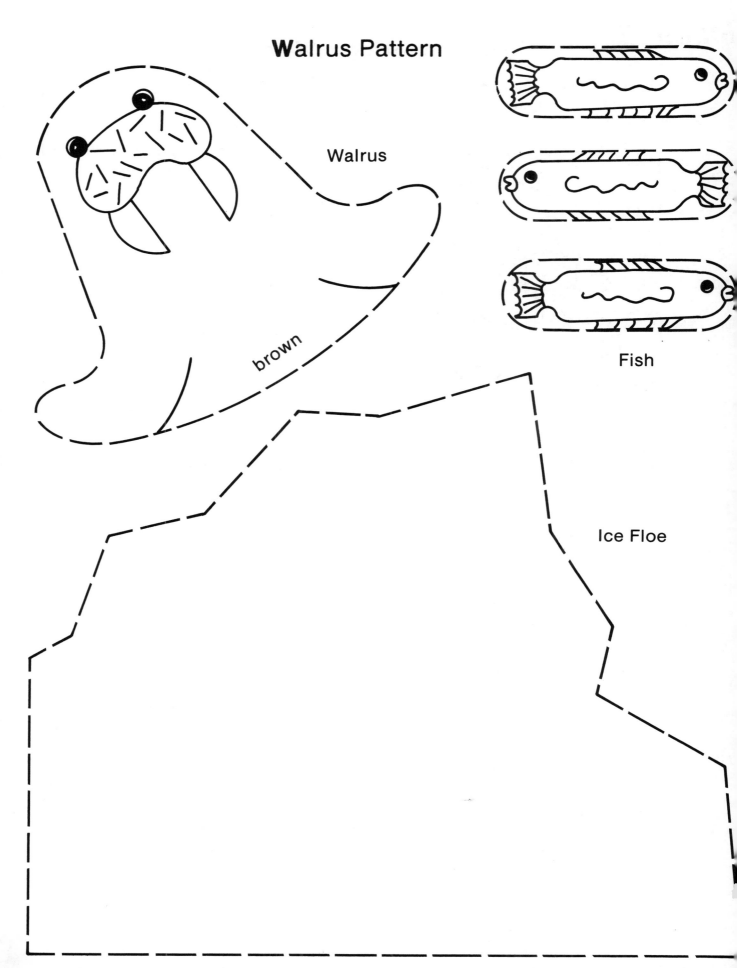

Walrus

brown

Fish

Ice Floe

FUN WITH THE ALPHABET

Xx

Read it!

1. *Adam's ABC* by Dale Fife
2. *The Fox* by Margaret Lane

Eat it!

Hot Cross Buns

X marks the top of these delicious buns.
Buy hot cross buns at the bakery. Children can add a more definite X using frosting. (Get the kind you squeeze out of little tubes.)

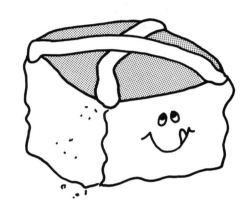

Draw it!

Direct students to fold a blank piece of paper into four sections. Draw on the chalkboard or use oral instructions to guide students to draw the following:

1. Make an ax with a red handle.
2. Make a box of red balls.
3. Make a jack-in-the-box.
4. Make a red fox.

Oral language Experience:
Students dictate a sentence or short story about one of the pictures to an adult.

Make it!

A Foxy Loxy Headband

All you need to make the head of
this little fox is a folded square of
construction paper.

Materials:

● Reproduce the tail pattern on
this page and the head
pattern on the following page
on white construction paper.

● 2- 12" x 3" white strips pasted
together to form the headband.

● Crayons, glue, stapler

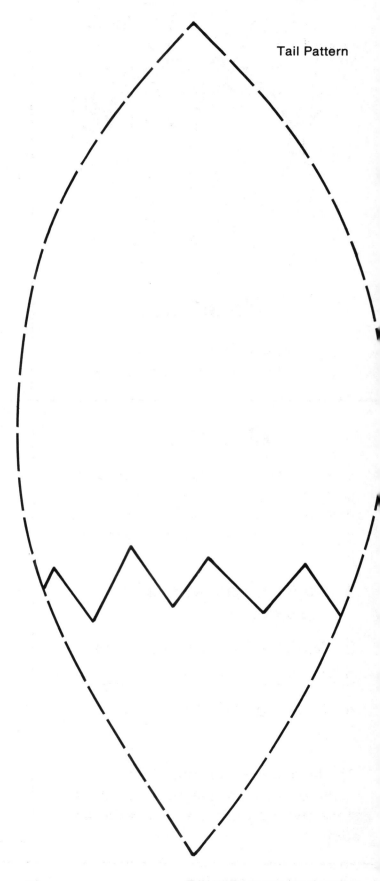

Tail Pattern

58   FUN WITH THE ALPHABET

Foxy Loxy Head Pattern

Steps to follow:

1. Cut out the head pattern.

2. Fold on the marked lines.

3. Color the fox's face red. Leave the ears white.

4. Cut out and color the tail.

white ── red

5. Staple the headband to fit each child's head.

6. Paste the head and tail pieces to the headband.

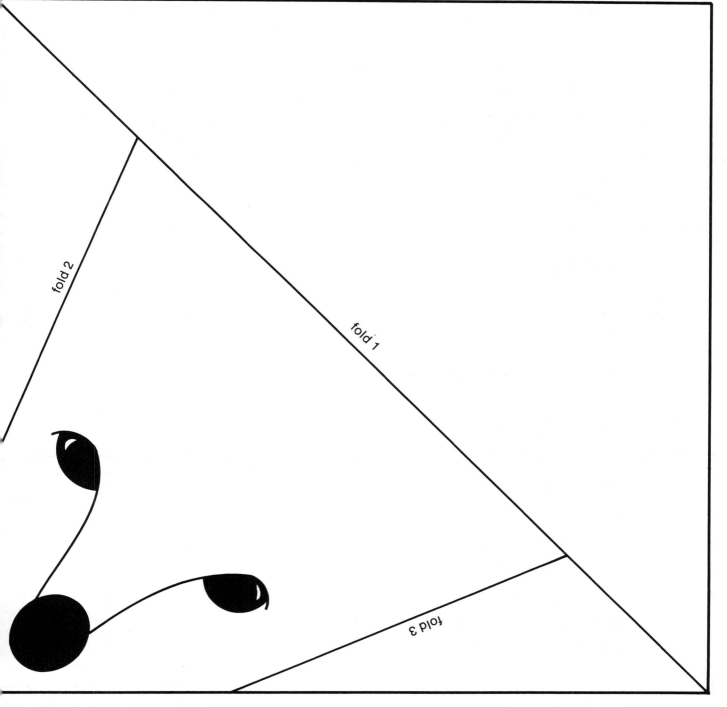

fold 2

fold 1

fold 3

 FUN WITH THE ALPHABET

Yy

Read it!

1. *Ape In A Cape* by Fritz Eichenberg
2. *Yankee Doodle* by Edward Bangs
3. *A New Treasure of Children's Poetry* by Joanna Cole has a whole section of poems on play and toys.

Eat it!

Yummy Yellow Yogurt

(Lemon Yogurt)

Have several flavors available for sampling. Be sure to include plain yogurt.

Play a tasting game. Blindfold a volunteer. Have the child taste all the kinds trying to find the "yummy yellow" one.

Draw it!

Direct students to fold a blank piece of paper into four sections. Draw on the chalkboard or use oral instructions to guide students to draw the following:

1. Make a purple yo-yo.
2. Make a little blue yo-yo.
3. Make a spinning green yo-yo.
4. Make a surprise yo-yo. Make it colorful.

Oral language Experience:
   Students dictate a sentence or short story about one of the pictures to an adult.

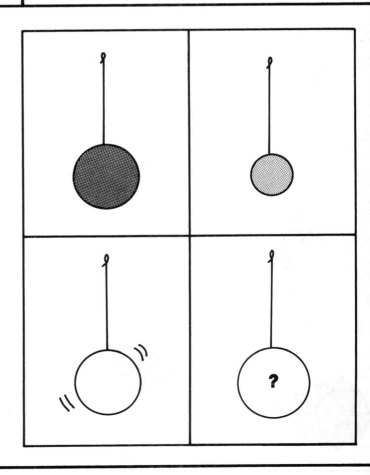

Make it!

Yankee Doodle Hat

Wear this hat and march around the room as you sing "Yankee Doodle". Let someone carry the flag as you march and sing.

Materials:

- 1- double sheet of news-paper trimmed down to a square.
- Scraps of construction paper to use in decorating your hat with feathers and medals.
- Paste, crayons

Steps to follow:

1. Fold the newspaper square:

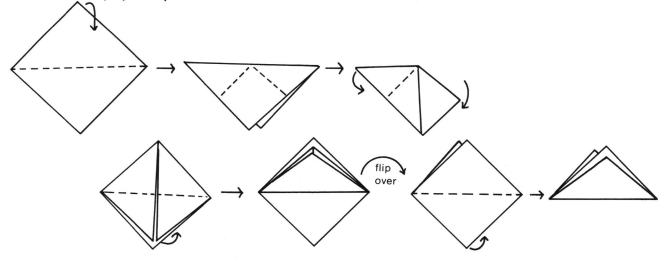

2. Paste the loose flaps to the main section of the hat.

3. Cut feathers from construction paper scraps to decorate the hat.

   Crayons may be used to add polka dots and stripes.

         FUN WITH THE ALPHABET

Zz

Read it!

1. *Albert B. Cub and Zebra, An Alphabetical Storybook* by Anne Rockwell

2. *Zebras* by Daphne Machin Goodall (Use the pages that are appropriate to your grade level.)

3. *Zippity Zap! A Book About Dressing* by Harriet Ziefert

Eat it!

Zucchini and Zippy Dip

Zucchini spears
Dip

Blend 2 cups of cottage cheese with a little milk until smooth. Add ½ cup of mayonaise and a package of your favorite dry salad dressing mix. Chill and serve with the zucchini spears.

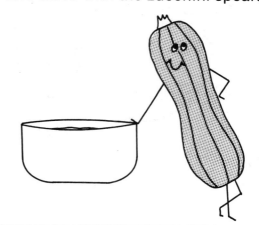

Draw it!

Direct students to fold a blank piece of paper into four sections. Draw on the chalkboard or use oral instructions to guide students to draw the following:

1. Make a zigzag across the box. Color it green.

2. Make a zigzag down the box. It looks like lightning in the sky. Make the sky blue.

3. Make a zigzag for a mouth. The boy looks unhappy.

4. Make a zigzag for a zipper.

Oral language Experience:
  Students dictate a sentence or short story about one of the pictures to an adult.

Make it!

Zippy, the Zoo Zebra

The zebra's stripes appear in many variations so the child may freely create his/her own design.

Materials:

- Reproduce the head pattern on the following page on white construction paper.

- 1-9" x 12" white construction paper for the body

- 8" strip of black yarn for a tail (knot both ends)

- crayons, paste

Steps to follow:

1. Fold the plain white construction paper in half. Hold the fold while cutting a half circle from the open side.

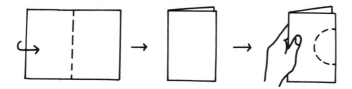

2. Draw and color zebra stripes on both sides of the body piece.

3. Cut out the head pattern and color the stripes. Fold on the fold line, and paste the head together.

4. Paste the finished head to one side of the zebra's body (inside).

   Paste the knotted yarn tail to the other end.

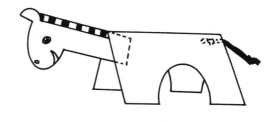

Display: Line your zebras up on a table along a strip of blue construction paper and watch them drink.

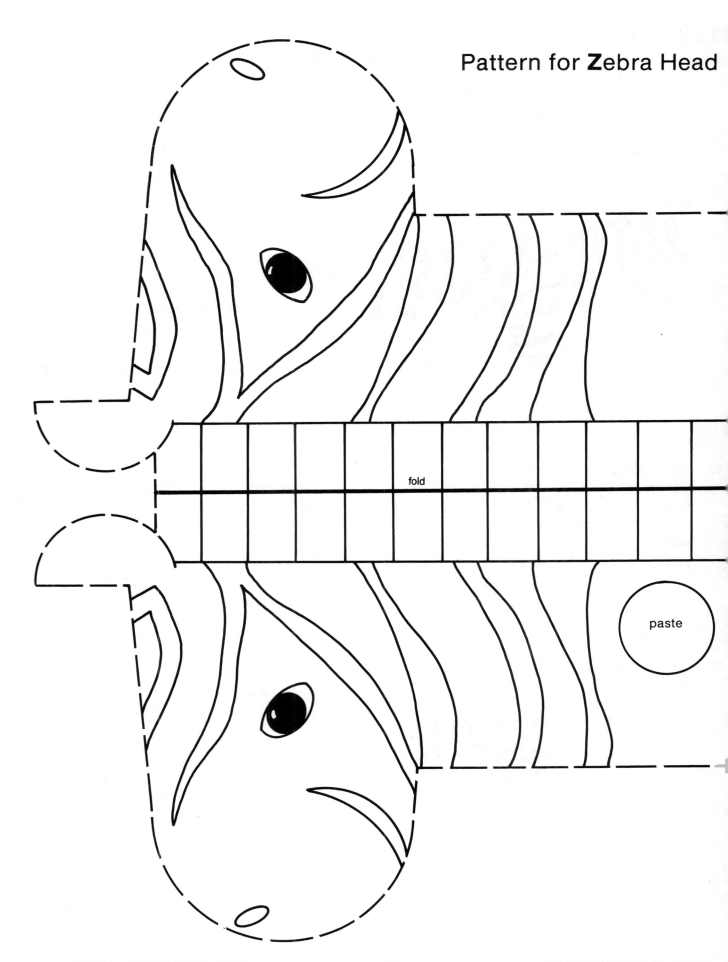

Pattern for **Z**ebra Head

fold

paste

64

FUN WITH THE ALPHABET